SIMPLE ETIQUETTE IN
FRANCE

By

Simple Books Ltd
Sandgate, Folkestone, Kent, England

SIMPLE ETIQUETTE IN FRANCE

Simple Books Ltd
Knoll House, 35 The Crescent, Sandgate, Folkestone,
Kent, England CT20 3EE

First published 1992
© Simple Books Ltd

ISBN 0-904404-81-1

British Library Cataloguing in Publication Data

**A CIP catalogue record for this book
is available from the British Library**

Distributed in the USA & Canada by:
THE TALMAN COMPANY, INC
150 Fifth Avenue
New York, NY 10011

Photoset in Souvenir Light 11 on 12pt
by Visual Typesetting, Harrow, Middlesex
Printed in England by BPCC Wheatons Ltd., Exeter

Contents

ACKNOWLEDGEMENTS

I would like to thank friends and relatives who gave me additional information promptly whenever it was necessary in the preparation of this book.

Foreword

France has a lot to offer. An extremely rich cultural heritage and a highly regarded cuisine provide pleasure both for the mind and the body. Your enjoyment should not be spoiled by trivial problems and misunderstandings and therefore I hope this book provides you with enough clear information to make such things as travelling around, shopping and ordering meals much easier. But it is just as important to the success of a visit to France to be able to get along with the French, and it is indeed essential if you are in France on business.

This book also sets out the basic rules which govern social exchanges in France; some understanding of them, therefore, will prevent you from offending people unwittingly. You will discover what the French consider as 'normal' but might appear strange to you. There is more than one way of doing things, so when in France, try to do as the French do: enjoy the countryside, the culture, the food and the wine. Your experiences may lead you to reassess what you always took for granted and discover your own culture from a different and unfamiliar angle. This is not only about discovering France and the French but also about discovering yourself.

MARIE-THÉRÈSE BYRAM
February 1992

1

Introducing France

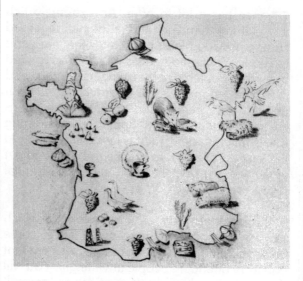

France is the largest country in Europe but with a population of only 55 million it is, in fact, one of the least densely populated. There are many large towns and cities but also vast rural areas with very few inhabitants and, in some regions, villages have been abandoned. In recent years, Europeans from more crowded countries such as Germany, Great Britain or the Netherlands have bought these abandoned houses, including many farmhouses, which are often situated in areas of breathtaking beauty.

The shape of France is roughly that of a hexagon and French people very often use this term when they refer to their country. Three of the sides, the North, the West and the South-West, face the sea. On the other sides it is separated from its neighbours by high mountains, except in the North-East where there are no natural boundaries.

There is a great diversity of landscape and variations in climate. In the northern and western parts the sea ensures mild winters but the eastern regions have a harsher climate of a more continental nature. On the Mediterranean coast people enjoy very mild winters but the summers can be unbearably hot.

Although France has been a unified and very centralised country for centuries, its regions have retained a great variety of culture, customs and culinary traditions.

For administrative purposes France is divided into 95 *départements* which are grouped into 22 *régions*. *Départements* are ordered alphabetically and numbered 1 to 95. These numbers are used as postal codes and as the last two digits of car registration numbers; for example 75 stands for Paris.

Départements were introduced after the 1789 revolution, but when asked where he comes from, a Frenchman will probably use the name of the pre-revolution province and proudly declare he was born in Brittany, Normandy or Provence, which are cultural entities. The names immediately conjure up a particular type of landscape, climate, traditions, specialities and way of speaking.

As in many countries, a North/South divide exists. Northerners think people from the *midi* (the South) talk and boast a lot, that they make friends very easily but that this friendliness

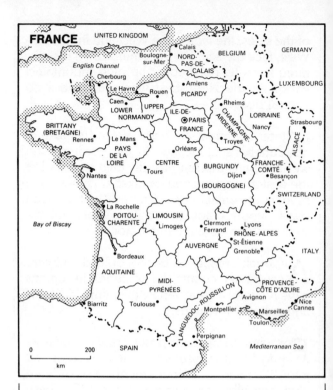

FRANCE

is somewhat superficial. They reckon the Southerners have a different conception of time and never hurry. On the other hand Southerners pity Northerners for living in what to them seems a cold climate which affects their character. *Les gens du Nord* are described as cold, hardworking, not very sociable and difficult to make friends with - but when a friendship develops, it is a deep and long-lasting relationship.

Although in recent years efforts have been made to give the regions a greater say in the running of their own affairs, the French administrative structure remains extremely centralised and hierarchical. However, it is a kind of national sport for the French to try and beat the system and avoid complying with decisions made in higher places. Behaviour which, in other countries, might be regarded as cheating, is looked on as perfectly acceptable. The attitude seems to be: Why should one obey silly regulations?

When confronted by officials, you are very often required to prove your identity and produce your passport, identity card, birth certificate or residence certificate. Foreigners should expect the same treatment as nationals, so you should keep your passport and driving licence with you at all times. Failure to produce your *papiers* when required by a policeman could well result in a visit to the local police station.

2

Meeting People

People shake hands when they meet and before parting again. It is usual for the senior person to proffer his or her hand first. If you enter a room where there are several people, shake hands with everyone; failing to shake hands might be interpreted as a sign of hostility, so it is important not to forget the handshake.

When you greet people, say: '*Bonjour, Monsieur*' to a man, '*Bonjour, Madame*' to a woman, '*Bonjour, Mademoiselle*' to a young lady.

The French tend to be rather formal and do not use first names easily. They might be friends and still address each other with '*Monsieur X*' or '*Madame Y*'. Things are changing with the younger generation, but to be on the safe side, never use the first name unless you have been expressly asked to do so; otherwise, it might be resented as being too familiar.

French people have two ways of addressing each other: the formal *vous*; or the more familiar *tu*, which is reserved for their family and close friends - or even colleagues in certain circles. But here again a word of warning. You might call a colleague of yours who is a friend by his first name and address him with *tu* when you are at home or alone, but you should revert to *Monsieur* and *vous* when you are back at work and in official meetings. The French tend not to mix their private life with the world of work.

Instead of shaking hands, relatives and close friends kiss each other (two, three or four times depending on the region where you are staying) but men keep to the handshake with other men.

Compared to Northern Europeans, French people are extrovert; their conversation is often reinforced by gestures. When taking part in a discussion in a group, they do not wait until someone has finished making a point, they inter-rupt and put forward their own ideas. This is not considered impolite; quick exchanges are the rule. If the discussion gets heated, the person who speaks or shouts loudest seems to win the argument. To an outsider this might appear aggressive, but not in the eyes of the French, who are brought up to be competitive and work against rather than with one another.

Conversation is frequently peppered with witty remarks. The French have a satirical sense of humour - but at other people's expense. If someone makes fun of them, they are touchy or even hurt; they consider it rude and defend themselves in an unexpectedly forceful manner.

It is said that foreigners, although they find French people friendly enough, are disappointed because they are not readily invited into French homes. The reason is that the French want only the best for their guests; everything has to be perfect, especially the food. Lunch or dinner offered to guests will invariably require considerable preparation which is one reason why a formal invitation may not happen straight away. But when it comes, it is a very special treat indeed. Be prepared to spend several hours at the dining table; for the French, a meal is the ideal social occasion, involving plenty of eating, drinking and talking.

French people are individualistic, insisting on doing things their own way even if it means bending the rules; but at the same time they seldom rebel against the constraints of family life.

Youngsters tend to stay at home much longer than their Northern European counterparts. Even when they start working, it is not unusual for them to stay with their parents until they marry. If they enter higher education, they attend the university nearest to their home. Children remain close to their grandparents, uncles, aunts and cousins. Sunday lunch, therefore, is invariably a family affair often including relatives living in the same district. This is especially the case in the provinces where families are not as scattered. French people are generally reluctant to move from one region to another even if job prospects are better; the only exception is moving from the provinces to Paris.

Traditionally France is a Catholic country but in recent times the church has lost a great deal of its influence. Although many people might not be church-goers, they still celebrate religious festivals which punctuate the different stages of life: birth, adolescence and marriage. *Baptême* for babies, *communion solennelle* for 12-year-olds and weddings are occasions for big family gatherings with huge meals lasting several hours.

With the arrival of many North African immigrants, Islam has become the second most important religion in France. There is also a Protestant minority which, despite being small in number, plays a fairly important role; many of its members occupy leading positions in politics or in the civil service. The population also includes a Jewish community.

In France, the older generation are not very good at speaking other languages. Foreign language teaching used to be very formal, based on learning grammar and the study of literary texts and not aimed at communicating effectively with foreigners. French was the language spoken by diplomats and educated foreigners visiting France. French people were not really keen on travelling and living abroad except perhaps in the French colonies; they were so confident in the superiority of everything French that they did not feel any need to communicate in another language.

Now attitudes and teaching methods have changed a great deal. Foreign language learning is encouraged at an early age, even at kindergarten and primary school. Youngsters are keen on acquiring foreign languages, mostly English, German, Spanish and to a lesser extent Italian and Russian. In many business schools English is compulsory and work experience abroad is highly valued.

Do not be upset if your attempts at communicating in French are thwarted by people talking back to you in English. It is mostly the case that they want to practise their skills and also make you feel at ease. Do not bear the French people a grudge, therefore, for not being able to use your French even in France! You will have plenty of other opportunities when French is the only means of communication and people will greatly appreciate the efforts you made to learn their language.

3

Business Contacts

French business people, especially the older generation, behave very formally. You are expected to dress smartly, shake hands with everybody, address individuals with the formal *vous* and use titles correctly. More and more young people speak English. Women are increasingly represented in the management of certain industries, particularly in Paris; but in the provinces they still have to fight prejudice.

In French companies the managing director (*PDG - President Directeur Génèral*) exercises control to an extent that some foreigners may find surprising. His authority is based on competence; he takes all the important decisions himself and his attitude to his subordinates is aloof.

If you wish to contact senior executives, do not rely too much on their 'secretary', who does not usually have the authority to make appointments.

Sometimes it may be difficult to organise meetings because French executives tend not to commit themselves until the last moment. Punctuality is expected of you, but you might have to wait if another engagement is considered more important than yours. Business appointments can be made during office hours, usually from 9 am to 6 pm. Some business people do not like to start the day in a hurry and will not see people before 9.30 am or even later. In the world of show business do not expect anything to happen before 11.30 am.

Business is still often done over an elaborate meal or perhaps during coffee at the end of it. The person who is trying to secure a contract pays for the meal. During negotiations you are expected to be clear, consistent and precise; things have to be logical to be accepted. French people appreciate abstract discussion and projects which are well thought out but do not care much for pragmatism. When drawing up contracts, the French side will insist in precision; a verbal agreement is only a preliminary to a written agreement, which alone is legally binding. As long as written documents have not been signed and exchanged, you cannot be sure of having secured anything.

Most people take their holidays in August, and it is therefore best avoided as far as promoting business is concerned.

The French style of letter writing is extremely formal. Do not be surprised if after a friendly meeting you receive a letter written in convoluted and impersonal language. The French are notorious for taking a long time in answering letters - if you need a prompt answer send a fax or telephone.

French Homes

Rented apartments rather than private houses are the norm in French towns and cities. The entrance to each apartment block used to be watched by the *concierge* or *gardien* who was in charge of distributing the mail and keeping the staircases clean, but in modern buildings you have to press the intercommunication button of the person you want to visit, state your name and he or she will open the main entrance by remote control. Individual doors are fitted with a brass plaque or a card carrying the name of the occupant.

The dream of every Frenchman is to have his own house built to his own specifications.

On new housing estates you will find a great variety of houses surrounded by a clearly delimited garden. However, in order not to spoil the character of an area, regulations put a curb on the individuality and creativity of French builders. Houses have to be in keeping with the traditional buildings of the region. For example in Brittany where roofs are covered with slates, it is prohibited to use tiles which are traditionally used in the South.

Many town-dwellers have a second home. Because of the exodus from rural areas, increasing numbers of village houses and farm buildings are deserted and bought as *résidences secondaires* where city-dwellers spend their weekends and holidays. You do not have to be very rich to afford these properties, except in the most sought-after areas in the South, where prices are high.

If you are invited into a French home, remember that the kitchen may be a no-go area. Do not insist on helping to carry things from the table or doing the washing-up; you would only embarrass your host or hostess who would probably think you were being nosy. They want you to enjoy a beautiful meal and the company but not to be aware of, or take part in, the hard work which goes on behind the scenes.

Eating and Drinking

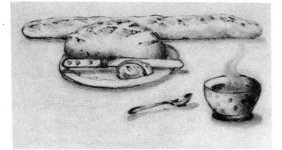

Two cooked meals a day - lunch and an evening meal - are usually eaten in France. For breakfast, coffee is drunk (often with milk) out of a bowl rather than a cup; children drink either white coffee or chocolate. White crispy bread is spread with butter and jam. Figure-conscious people eat *biscotte*, a kind of toasted bread. On Sundays, the first one up buys freshly baked *croissants*.

Lunch-time usually lasts for two hours and whenever possible the whole family comes together. As schoolchildren start work at 8.30 am and finish at 4.30 pm or later, schools provide a canteen to cater for those who cannot go home.

Lunch usually consists of a main course which might be meat or fish and vegetables, preceded by a starter and followed by lettuce, cheese and/or a dessert. There is always a basket of bread on the table as French people eat bread throughout the meal, except with soup. However tempting fresh, crispy bread might be, refrain from nibbling at a piece before the meal actually starts or between courses, or your host will think you are desperately hungry.

Always break the bread with your fingers, never cut it. There are no side plates for bread, so do not worry if crumbs go all over the table. It is often assumed that the French use bread to clean their plates. Although they might occasionally indulge in this practice privately at home in order to eat a particularly delicious sauce, doing it in the presence of guests is considered bad manners.

When children return from school, they have *goûter* which consists of a piece of bread with a bar of chocolate or a pastry.

Most people finish work at 6 pm, consequently the evening meal does not start until 7 or 8 pm. The whole family gathers around the dinner table, even young children, and might well listen to or watch the news broadcast.

On Sundays, more members of the extended family may be reunited and meals are more elaborate. They are preceded by an *aperitif*, a drink like Martini, whisky, a typically French *pastis* (a drink flavoured with aniseed) or *Suze* (a bitter drink made with herbs).

Starters consist of salads, *charcuterie* (cold sliced meat and sausages) or shellfish. A special meal might have two main courses. Vegetables are sometimes served on their own after the main course. Refrain from using the salt and pepper cellars even if they are on the table; adding more spices would imply that the person who prepared the meal did not get it right. To refresh the palate a lettuce tossed in oil and vinegar is served, followed by cheese. The meal ends with the dessert: cake or ice-cream for example, and fruit.

People linger at the table, drink coffee and *digestifs* such as Cognac, Calvados (apple brandy) or *liqueurs* for the ladies: Cointreau or Grand Marnier (orange based), Chartreuse or Bénédictine (made with herbs). If you are a smoker, this is when you may light a cigarette. It would be very rude to smoke during the meal as it prevents you and others from properly tasting and appreciating the food the host or hostess has spent hours preparing.

WINE

Wine is the traditional drink. If it is ordinary table wine, it might be diluted with water to quench the thirst but if it is good quality wine, it is drunk straight in little sips. As soon as your glass is empty, it will be replenished; if you do not want to drink a lot, always leave something in your glass. Drinking and enjoying wine is an art. For the experience to be perfect, wine has to have the right colour, smell and taste, and be at the right temperature.

Although tap water is all right, French people insist on drinking bottled water. In a restaurant if you want to avoid the expense of mineral water (which can be very pricey) ask for *une carafe d'eau*, tap water which is provided free.

Different wines are served during the meal: *rosé* or *blanc sec* (dry white) with starters, *rouge* (red) with meat, dry white with fish, *blanc doux* (sweet white) with the dessert. Before drinking wipe your lips with your napkin and hold your glass by the stem in order not to leave marks on the glass which would prevent you from fully appreciating the colour and quality of the wine. The French can be lyrical about wine; they have very many words to describe the colour, smell and taste.

The pattern of a French meal always remains the same, but the content can vary tremendously depending on the area. Due to its varied geography and climate, France has a great variety of products which are used in rich and original regional cuisines. Normandy is famous for its specialities cooked in cream and apple brandy, Brittany for its seafood, Burgundy for dishes cooked in wine, Périgord for poultry preserved in its own fat and dishes flavoured with truffles, Provence for dishes including olive oil, garlic, tomatoes and peppers. Northern areas use butter and onions, southern areas oil and garlic in their cooking. Although wine is drunk everywhere in France, cider is the traditional drink in the West and beer in the East and extreme North.

Important events of a private nature are celebrated with a special meal. Christmas and New Year, of course, are also occasions for a big meal: *le réveillon*. Traditionally oysters, which are then at their best, are served as starters, followed by a special choice of *charcuterie* which might well include *foie gras* (goose or duck liver preserved in fat). The main course is turkey served with chestnuts, followed by lettuce, a choice of cheeses and a cake shaped like a log. The *réveillon* takes place on Christmas Eve, and gifts are also exchanged between members of the family. New Year's Eve is a similar occasion often celebrated with friends rather than relatives.

French people are immensely proud of their cooking and wine; they are convinced that nothing is better. Even if your grasp of French is limited, be sure you show your appreciation of a meal by your facial expression - or by taking second helpings! Then you will be regarded as good company and worth inviting again.

Be ready to taste new food; declining to sample a dish prepared by your host would be very rude. If you can speak some French, do not hesitate to ask questions about the food being served; beside consuming food, talking about it is a favourite French pastime. In doing so, your reputation will be greatly enhanced and you will be respected as a foreigner who understands what really matters at the same time.

If you are invited for a meal, arrive promptly; the different stages will have been carefully timed, so do not put all the efforts of the cook at risk by arriving late. It is customary to present flowers to the hostess, but not chrysanthemums which in France are associated with death (they are put on graves on 1 November). Choose an odd number of flowers but avoid 13. A box of chocolates is also a traditional gift. Bringing a bottle of wine is not a good idea, as it could be interpreted as a lack of confidence in the ability of your host to provide enough good drink. A bottle of high quality spirit, however, is quite acceptable.

A meal is not just about food - conversation is almost as important. In a festive meal which can last several hours, there is plenty of time for discussion between courses. Although no topic is really taboo, talking about money is not welcome; asking a person how much he/she earns or what has been paid for a certain item would cause embarrassment.

WHERE TO EAT AND DRINK

A great range of restaurants can be found throughout France. You do not have to spend a lot of money to obtain a good meal. To a certain extent, the prices can reflect the quality of service rather than that of the food provided. For example in the lower price range, the cutlery probably will not be changed with every course. The menu and prices are displayed outside restaurants. Occasionally, in exclusive restaurants ladies are handed menus without prices, a custom left over from the times when women were always entertained and not supposed to know at what cost.

It is worth trying smaller places specialising in regional cooking but if you are in a hurry, do as the French do and order a *steak frites* (steak and chips). When ordering steak, keep in mind that to a French cook *saignant* (rare) means that the steak is just sealed on both sides. If you like your meat pink ask for *à point* or *bien cuit* if you cannot face under-cooked meat.

O ften it is better value to choose a *menu* (set menu) rather than *à la carte*. A set menu might include wine, whereas a very reasonably-priced meal can become much more expensive when you order wine separately as restaurateurs make most of their profits on drinks. If you are not sure which wine would be appropriate for a particular dish, ask for advice - the restaurateur will take pride in choosing the right wine for you. If you decided to order something completely unsuitable, such as red wine with fish for example, he probably would not be able to resist putting you right anyway.

If you are travelling and want to stop for a meal on the main road, *Routiers* restaurants are to be recommended. They cater mainly (but not exclusively) for long-distance drivers, providing good and very substantial meals at a reasonable price. The longer the queue of articulated lorries in the car park, the better the food is likely to be.

Brasseries also provide meals but the choice of dishes is not as great as in restaurants. You are expected to order a full meal in a restaurant but in a brasserie ordering just the main course is fine.

Creperies are places which specialise in pancakes, sweet and savoury. In Brittany and Normandy the pancakes are accompanied by delicious sparkling cider served in bowls.

Cafés are convivial places where friends meet, chat and watch the world go by. They are open from early morning until late at night, serving not only coffee but also alcoholic and soft drinks; one favourite is *citron pressé* freshly squeezed lemon juice with water, ice-cube and sugar to taste served in a large glass.

Cafés also prepare snacks: sandwiches with *jambon* (ham), *saucisson* (cold sausage), *rillette* (pork spread), *fromage* (cheese) or a hot *croque monsieur* (slice of toasted bread with ham and cheese).

Remember that if you decide to sit outside on the terrace, drinks will be more expensive than when you stand at the counter. Service is normally included in the price, but the waiter still expects a tip (*pourboire*).

Cafés-Tabac, which display a red carrot-shaped sign outside, not only sell tobacco but also stamps, phonecards and, in Paris, Metro/bus tickets.

6

Travelling Around

DRIVING IN FRANCE

If you drive in France, remember the following speed limits:

130 kph (80 mph) on motorways;
90 kph (55 mph) on other roads;
50 kph (30 mph) in built-up areas.

Not all French drivers observe these limits, but if they are caught speeding, there are on-the-spot fines. A solidarity has developed among drivers and if you see a vehicle coming in the opposite direction flashing its headlights, it is a warning that *gendarmes* (policemen) are not far away, and for a few miles motorists will adjust their speed and behave as exemplary drivers.

Furthermore, French drivers tend not to be too considerate towards pedestrians either - even at pedestrian crossings. In order to remedy this, speed ramps are being introduced. They are made so high that it would ruin the suspension of your car if you were to drive over them at more than 20 kph. At last pedestrians in France have a chance to cross the roads in some degree of safety!

As a rule you have to give way to traffic coming from the right, even if you are on a main road. If you see a white post with a red line at the end of a farm track, theoretically you have to give way to vehicles emerging from this track.

Roundabouts are becoming more numerous but there seem to be no uniform rules as to who has right of way. When you arrive at a roundabout, a sign will advise you if you can proceed or not; *Cedez le passage* or *vous n'avez pas la priorité* indicates you have to give way to traffic already on the roundabout.

Except for short sections around towns, French motorways are *autoroutes à péage*, toll motorways. You pay at the entrance by throwing coins into a kind of basket or pushing them into a slot, or you are given a ticket and pay at the exit. It is also possible to use credit cards. The motorway network is relatively new in France and very often large sections run parallel to the *routes nationales* (main roads) which are very good and signposted with N followed by a number; D roads are *routes départmentales* which are narrower.

Driving in Paris can be very frustrating because of the one-way system and the lack of parking spaces. Parisians have developed an amazing skill at parking in the smallest gap, great use being made of bumpers to enlarge the space between two parked cars. In the centre most parking spaces are *payant*, with a high hourly rate in an attempt to encourage commuters to use public transport rather than their own cars. August is the only time when driving in Paris is easy - because so many Parisians are away on holiday.

If you want to avoid driving through Paris, use the *Boulevard Péripherique* (the ring road). However, at peak hours it can be heavily congested, so make sure you stay in the right-hand lane (the slow lane) in order not to miss your exit. Many sections of the *Péripherique* were built on what were once the fortifications of Paris, and most exits are called *Porte de...* which means 'gate'.

Driving on main roads is best avoided on public holidays during the summer. As most people take their holidays in July and August, on the first and last weekend of these months traffic is at its worst, with long tailbacks near large cities.

In an attempt to reduce drinking and driving, police apply the law rigorously, and driving licences can be withdrawn on the spot.

The wearing of seatbelts is compulsory and it is illegal to have a child in the front seat either strapped in or on the passenger's lap.

RAILWAYS

Trains are cheap, reliable and clean but they tend to be crowded at weekends and during public holidays. On these occasions it is advisable to book your seat in advance.

PUBLIC HOLIDAYS

New Year
Easter and Easter Monday
1 May
Ascension Day in May
Pentecôte (Whitsun) at the end of May
14 July, National Day
15 August, Assumption Day
1 November, All Saints' Day
11 November, Remembrance Day
25 December, Christmas Day

It is compulsory to book your seat in advance on the TGV (*Train de Grande Vitesse* - high-speed train).

The SNCF (French Railways) makes great efforts to please customers, besides making sure that trains run on time. Trains are clean and the seats are pleasant and comfortable. In *trains corail* (express trains) there is a special carriage where children can play, and during the summer, entertainment is provided on the main lines at no extra cost. A carriage can house an exhibition, a cinema, become a stage for artists or offer you specialities of the region you are travelling through.

Before boarding a train you must validate your ticket by pushing it into a small machine which punches a hole and stamps the date. There are frequent ticket inspections on trains and inspectors speak foreign languages, so you cannot easily get away with pretending you do not understand.

In France coaches are not an alternative to trains, they only go where trains do not go.

PUBLIC TRANSPORT IN PARIS

The *Metro* (underground) is the cheapest and fastest way to travel in Paris. Each line takes its name from the last stop, which means that on a return journey the same line will have a different name. If you have to change, follow the sign *Correspondance* and the appropriate name of the line.

It is cheaper to buy a booklet of 10 tickets, so ask for a *carnet*. These tickets can also be used on buses. They can be bought not only at Metro stations but also at newsagents and Cafés-Tabac. On the Metro you only need one ticket whatever the length of your journey and irrespective of the number of times you change lines.

On buses you need tickets according to the length of your journey and you have to pay again whenever you board a new bus. Some bus lines can be a cheap alternative to sightseeing tours as they take you past the main sights. This is true of line 72 between the Hotel de Ville (Town Hall) and the Eiffel Tower, for example.

Keep your ticket until you leave the bus or Metro as you might be required to produce it for inspection.

Try avoiding the rush hours (between 7 and 9 in the morning, 6 and 7.30 in the evening) when it would be difficult to extricate yourself and your luggage from the carriage and you would be unpopular with fellow passengers. Luggage is not accepted on buses at any time. Queuing is virtually unknown at bus stops, so it is necessary to assert yourself - sometimes with vigorous use of the elbows.

7

Out and About

As in other parts of Europe, large shopping centres and supermarkets are replacing small shops, but French people still rely on corner shops and markets for certain types of food. The French like their bread fresh and crisp, and in towns they are prepared to go twice a day to the baker's shop which opens at 7.30 am and remains open until 7 or 8 pm; it even opens until noon on Sundays. Other shops open later, at 8 or 9 am, but all of them are shut for two or three hours at midday.

When you pay for goods in France, do not try to put the money directly into the cashier's hands; use the little rubber mat or glass dish on the counter.

POST OFFICES

Hours of business are usually between 8 am and 7 pm on weekdays and until 12 noon on Saturdays. Stamps can also be obtained from Bars-Tabac. Letter-boxes are yellow.

The public phone system in France is very comprehensive and includes even the smallest villages. Coin-operated phones are still available, but in large towns most public phones require a *télécarte* (phonecard). If you intend spending some time in France it might be worth buying a *télécarte* with 50 *unités*. You can buy *télécartes* at post offices, railway stations, Bars-Tabac (with the red carrot sign) and some newsagents.

If you want to phone abroad, first dial 19 and wait for a dialling tone; then - and only then - dial the country code followed by the number of the person you are calling. If the phone number begins with a zero, omit it when dialling.

BANKS

Most banks are open between 9 am and 12 noon, and from 2 pm to 4 pm on weekdays; and from 9.30 am to 12 noon on Saturdays. In certain areas they are closed all day on Saturday or Monday. They are closed on Sundays and public holidays.

Museums and monuments are usually closed all day on Tuesdays.

PETROL STATIONS

Sometimes attendants are reluctant to accept cheques or even refuse them for amounts over 100 francs; but credit cards are acceptable.

WHERE TO STAY

The *Office du Tourisme* or *Syndicat d'initiative* (Tourist Information Office) will help you in choosing from a range of hotels rated from one star to four stars.

Usually you pay for the room rather than per person, and breakfast is not included. Some hotels which also run restaurants expect you to have a meal there if you want a room, although such a requirement is not legal.

If you wish to stay in a Bed and Breakfast establishment look for the sign *Chambre d'hôtes*. In the countryside *Table d'hôtes* might be on offer as well; this means you can have a meal and take the opportunity to sample local specialities at a reasonable price.

If you plan a longer stay in an area, *gîtes* are an interesting option. These are self-catering holiday homes, very often old farmhouses or houses of character which have been renovated.

Youth Hostels, *Auberges de Jeunesse*, are not generally as numerous as in certain other European countries, although this depends on the area.

PUBLIC CONVENIENCES

The famous freestanding urinals are now museum pieces and have been replaced by unobtrusive unisex cabins. Green and red lights have replaced the *libre* or *occupé* signs. The door opens when you push coins into a slot.

Some public toilets have attendants who will not let you go in unless you put the required amount of money in a little dish. French people are surprised by the reluctance of some foreigners to use *toilettes turques*; they cannot see what all the fuss is about. Instead of having a toilet seat, you stand on slightly raised footrests and squat. Just make sure you unlock the door and are ready to exit swiftly before you flush the toilet.

If no public toilets are available, you can go into a café; they will not mind you using their facilities if you leave a tip.

8

Useful Words and Phrases

WORDS YOU ALREADY KNOW

Hotel, restaurant, banque, taxi, poste, téléphone, toilette, bus.

SIGNS

entrée	entrance
déviation	diversion
sortie	exit
péage	toll
interdit	prohibited
douane	Customs
défense de ...	prohibited
gare	railway station
non fumeur	non-smoking
hommes	gentlemen
femmes	ladies
cédez le passage	give way
vous n'avez pas la priorité	give way

WHAT YOU CAN SAY

oui	yes
non	no
pardon	excuse me
bonjour	good morning/day
bonsoir	good evening
au revoir	goodbye
s'il vous plait	please
parlez-vous anglais?	do you speak English?
comment?	I beg your pardon
je ne comprends pas	I don't understand
où est...?	where is...?
quand?	when?
c'est combien?	how much is it?
une chambre	a room
avec douche	with shower
avec salle de bain	with bathroom

WHAT YOU MIGHT HEAR

Bon séjour	Have a nice stay
Bon voyage	Have a good journey
Bonne année	Happy New Year
Joyeux Noël	Merry Christmas

9

Did You Know..?

French is spoken by 55 million people in France, and is a first language in Belgium and Switzerland. It is also widely used outside Europe: in the Quebec province of Canada, in North Africa and many countries of West Africa, in Madagascar and Mauritius, the West Indies (Martinique, Guadeloupe and Haiti), South America (French Guiana) and South East Asia (Vietnam and Cambodia).

Liberté, Égalité, Fraternité is the motto of the French Republic, which you will see written on public buildings and coins.

Marianne is the symbol of the French Republic, a female figure found on stamps and coins. Every town hall has a bust of her, modelled on a famous French woman, from Brigitte Bardot in the sixties to a Chanel model in the eighties.

On 14 July, France's national day, people celebrate the storming of the Bastille, which until 1789 was a fortress where the monarch could imprison anyone at will. A big military parade takes place on the Champs Elysées, the most prestigious avenue in Paris, and throughout France it is celebrated with dances and firework displays.

Most families send their children to state schools which are free and considered to provide the best education. The majority go to nursery schools before they reach compulsory school age. Wednesday is a free day for schoolchildren but many have lessons on Saturday morning. The French education system is very competitive; children have to repeat a class if they have not achieved a certain level by the end of the school year. The National Curriculum issued by the Ministry of Education prescribes in detail what has to be learned.

The French take great pride in their long and prestigious literary tradition. However, in schools literature is not considered as important as mathematics, an ability which is generally used as a gauge of intelligence, perhaps because it demands skills in logical thinking.

In higher education, universities are open to anyone who has passed the *Baccalaureat* (secondary education leaving certificate) but there is also a system of highly selective *Grandes Écoles* where many top executives, civil servants and politicians are educated.

Since the beginning of the twentieth century church and state have been strictly separated and religion is not taught in state schools.

Every young man over 18 must do military service, although the length of time is being reduced more and more and civil community service can be done instead. In this case the conscript spends ten months working as a fireman, helping in a hospital or work related to the protection of the environment.

In summer, the French like playing *boules*. The aim is to roll solid steel balls as close as possible to a little wooden ball, the *cochonnet*. You can throw them to try and dislodge an opponent's ball. Any patch of ground will do, from a village square to a garden path.

Cycling is very popular. The famous Tour de France race is followed by millions during July. The final stage ends on the Champs Elysées in Paris and the winner wears a yellow vest, the coveted *maillot jaune*.

In winter, an increasing number of people go to ski resorts in the Alps or the Pyrenées. Since the law entitles employees to five weeks paid holiday each year, people tend to take three or four weeks in summer, keeping a week or two for a winter break. Thanks to *classes de neige* (snow classes), children from all over France have the chance to enjoy winter sports. Whole classes go to a resort with their teachers, do schoolwork in the morning and spend the afternoon skiing.

France has a long and varied coastline which attracts many holiday-makers who are keen on water sports. But you do not have to be at the seaside to go sailing, water-skiing or windsurfing. Local authorities have made great efforts to develop the potential of lakes and have created numerous artificial ones. They might be modest in size but they allow people to enjoy water sports and restore a balance in the environment in areas where modern methods of agriculture had led to the disappearance of a particular flora and fauna.

In order to attract the tourist industry, regional authorities have renovated waterways which had fallen into neglect when rail and road traffic became more profitable. Hiring a barge or a small boat is now an available option for people who wish to explore a region in an unusual and relaxing way.

French people are immensely proud of their cultural heritage; they even have a Ministry for Culture. In summer many theatre and music festivals are organised in the provinces. Ancient monuments are used as the setting for plays and concerts even in remote areas. Floodlit castles are the venue for *Sons et Lumiere* - elaborate performances during which local actors recreate historical events.

The French take cinema very seriously and call it the 'seventh art'. French film-makers concentrate on analysing human relationships within the family or a small group of people rather than aiming for spectacular productions.

Jazz music is an important genre in France. In recent years, popular music has been enriched by musical traditions from Africa, in the same way as plastic arts were greatly influenced by African art in the twenties. A strong tradition of *chansons* is still thriving, in which songs are similar to poems and the words matter more than the accompanying music.

In recent years French presidents have attempted to leave their mark on society by commissioning large projects, for example Georges Pompidou with the Pompidou Centre, or Beaubourg, a futuristic multimedia and exhibition centre in Paris, or François Mitterrand with the new Opera Bastille. To have one's name linked with a cultural achievement is considered the ultimate in personal prestige.

The *Légion d'honneur* created by the Emperor Napoleon is still one of France's greatest honours. It is conferred for services rendered to the nation. People who have received this honour wear a tiny red button in their lapel.

VOCAB/MEMO

SIMPLE ETIQUETTE IN
FRANCE

ILLUSTRATED BY
ANNIE WALEY